What goes in Karol's bookbag? Trace each path to find out.

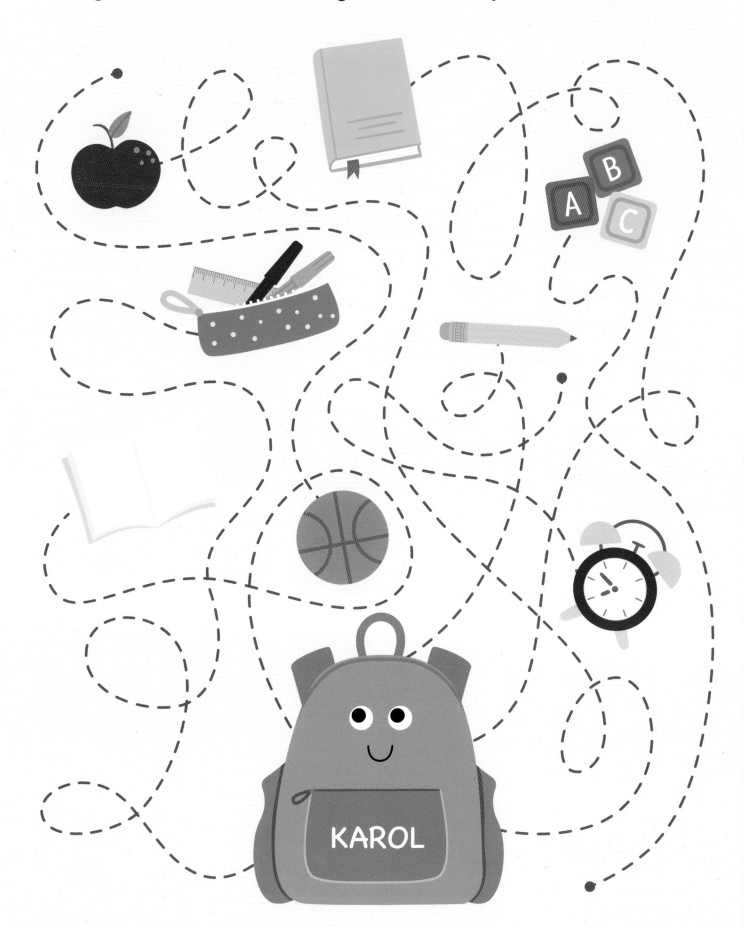

Trace and write.

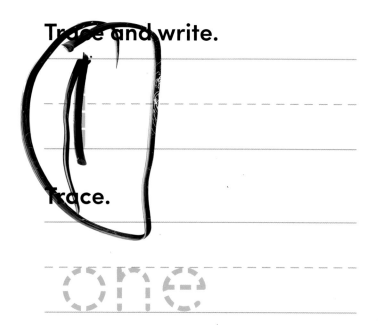

Trace.

one

two

Circle 1 and 2.

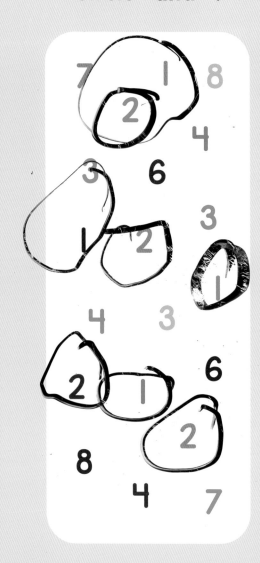

Complete each sentence. Write 1 or 2.

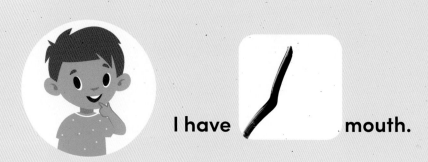
I have ___ mouth.

I have ___ eyes.

I have ___ nose.

Trace and write.

Trace.

Draw toppings on the slice of pizza to make Tarik's order.
Then, wipe clean to make Zoe's order.

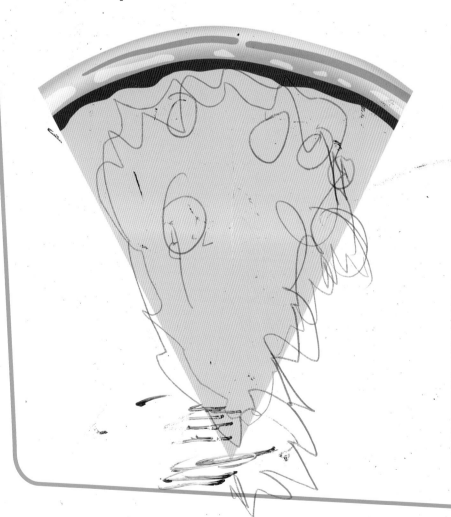

Tarik's Order

3 pepperoni

4 mushrooms

Zoe's Order

4 pineapple

3 basil leaves

Trace and write.

Trace.

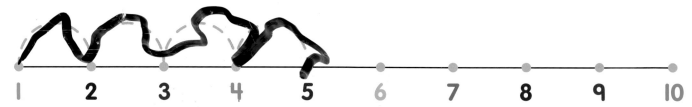

Trace the number line to count to 5.

| 1 | 2 | 3 | 4 | 5 | 6 | 7 | 8 | 9 | 10 |

Count the stars. Draw or add stickers to make 5 stars.

4

Circle 8 differences.

Trace and write.

Trace.

Trace the number line to count to 6.

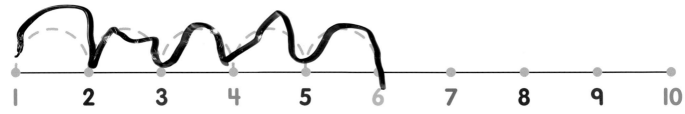

1 2 3 4 5 6 7 8 9 10

Circle each cow with 6 spots.

6

Trace and write.

7

Trace.

seven

Trace the number line to count to 7.

1   2   3   4   5   6   7   8   9   10

Draw 7 cherries on the banana split.

Trace and write.

Trace.

eight

Trace the number line to count to 8.

| 1 | 2 | 3 | 4 | 5 | 6 | 7 | 8 | 9 | 10 |

Trace each 8 on the ice.

Trace and write.

Trace.

Trace the number line to count to 9.

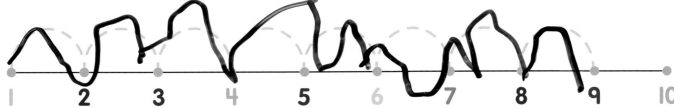

1   2   3   4   5   6   7   8   9   10

Draw 9 cookies on the plate.

Trace and write.

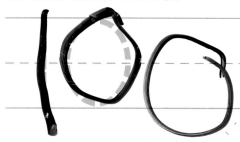

Trace.

Trace the number line to count to 10.

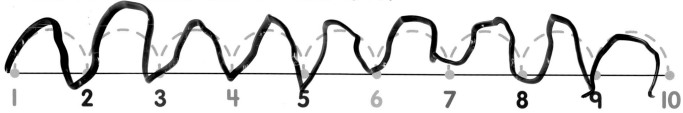

| 1 | 2 | 3 | 4 | 5 | 6 | 7 | 8 | 9 | 10 |

Count the seashells. Draw or add stickers to make 10 seashells.

10

Count each animal. Write the number.

8 2 1 4 10

Trace and write.

11

Trace.

eleven

Draw a dot in 11 boxes.

Draw toppings on the ice cream to make Ava's order. Then, wipe clean to make Sahil's order.

11 gummy worms

11 candy hearts

Trace and write.

12

Trace.

twelve

Draw a dot in 12 boxes.

Use the decoder to add numbers to the clock below.

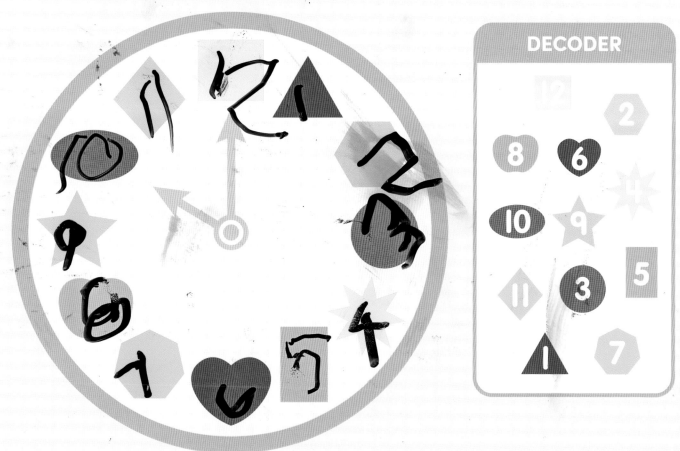

DECODER

Trace and write.

13

Trace.

thirteen

Draw a dot in 13 boxes.

Count each group of seashells.
Trace the path from each group to its matching number.

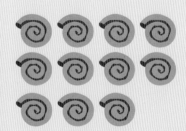  

13   11   12

14

Trace and write.

14

Trace.

fourteen

Draw a dot in 14 boxes.

Find and circle 14 orange and white clownfish.

Trace and write.

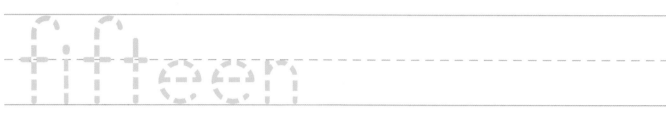

Trace.

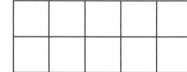

Draw a dot in 15 boxes.

Make a snowman! Connect the dots from 1 to 15.

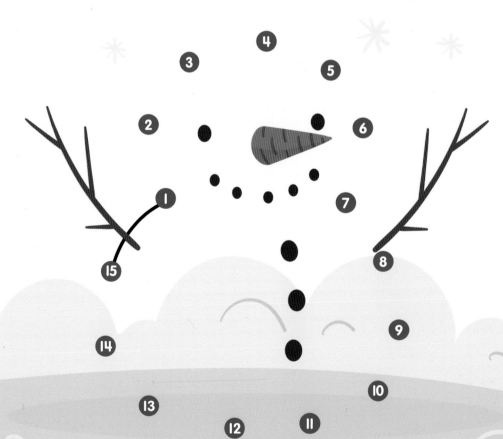

16

Chef Stella wants to make a salad. Which jar has all the correct ingredients? Circle the correct jar.

Ingredients

2 strawberries
5 lettuce leaves
4 tomato slices
3 orange slices
6 cucumber slices
½ of an avocado

Trace and write.

16

Trace.

sixteen

Draw a dot in 16 boxes.

Match each number and word to the correct group of marbles.

12   sixteen

16   eleven

11   twelve

Trace and write.

17

Trace.

seventeen

Draw a dot in 17 boxes.

Count the gems in each tray. Circle the one with 17 gems.

Trace and write.

18

Trace.

eighteen

Draw a dot in 18 boxes.

Help the golfer finish the course. Draw a line to connect all the golf balls with the number 18.

START

18   18   11   16

7   18   13   18   15

18   8   18   18

10   18   18   9   18

END

Trace and write.

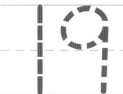

Trace.

Draw a dot in 19 boxes.

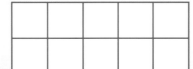 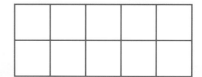

Circle the leaf with 19 insects.

Trace and write.

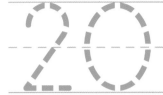

Trace.

Match each number and word to the correct group of butterflies.

17 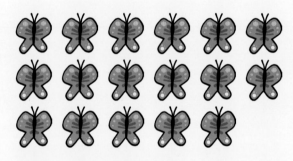 fifteen

15  twenty

20  seventeen

Write the missing numbers.

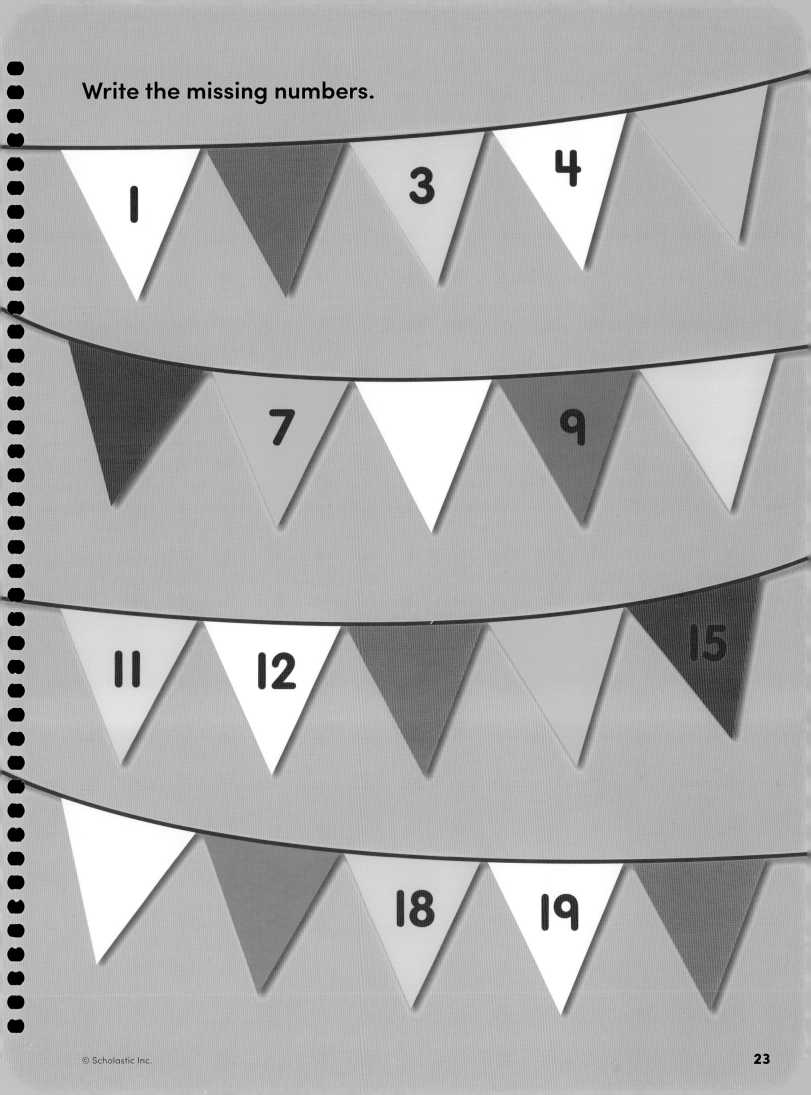

1 _ 3 4 _

_ 7 _ 9 _

11 12 _ _ 15

_ _ 18 19 _

Connect the dots from 1 to 20.

Mama Hen has lost her chicks. Find and circle 10 chicks.

Place a matching sticker on each smiley face below. Then, add. Write the answer in the box.

How many kites are in each group? Write your answer.
Then, add the two groups of kites in each row.

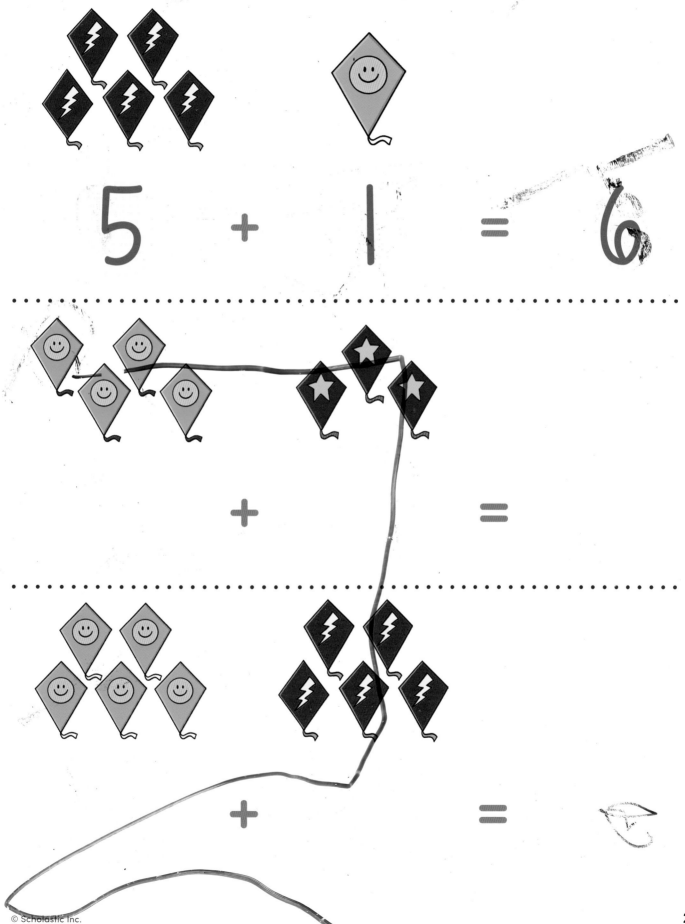

$$5 \ + \ 1 \ = \ 6$$

© Scholastic Inc.

Circle the flock that has more birds.

Circle the animal that has fewer spots.

28

What would each cake look like from above?
Draw a line to match each cake to the correct top view.

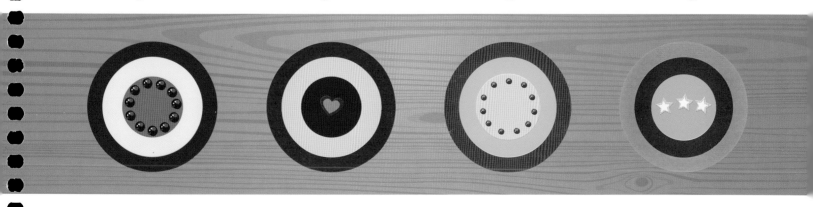

Circle the two ice cream cones that are the same.

Trace each A and a.

Ant likes apples.

Help Ant get to the apples!
Follow the items that begin with the A sound.

Trace each B and b.

Ben buys a bike.

Circle the items that begin with the B sound.

Trace each C and c.

Cats are cute.

Connect the dots from 1 to 10.

What did you make? Write c to complete the sentence.

I made a ___at.

Trace each D and d.

Dogs dance.

Match each dog to its twin. Then, write D on each dog.

Trace each E and e.

Ed exercises.

Find and circle each E and e in the picture.

How many did you find?   E   e

Trace each F and f.

Frogs fish for fun.

Connect the dots from Ⓐ to Ⓕ and ⓐ to ⓕ.

What did the frogs catch? Write f to complete each word.

___ork   ___lower

Circle the robot that is unique.

Trace each G and g.

Gia gets a goal.

Follow the path with G to help Gia get a goal.

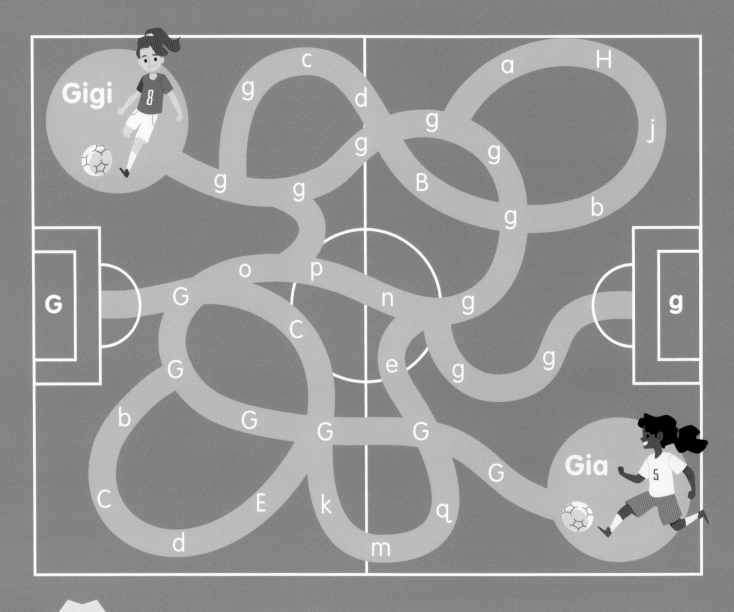

MORE FUN — Wipe the picture clean. Then, follow the path with **g** to help **Gigi** score!

Trace each H and h.

Hippo has a hat.

Draw a hat on the hippo. Write H on the hat.

Trace each I and i.

Inez is an insect.

Write I to complete each insect's name. Then, find and circle Inez.

___an

___ra

___mani

___dris

___nez

___rene

40

Trace each J and j.

Jon juggles.

Circle the jelly beans with the letters J and j.

Trace each K and k.

Kids like kites.

Trace the lines to match each child to a kite.
Then, write **K** on each kite.

Trace each L and l.

Lee likes lollipops.

Circle the items that begin with the L sound.

Trace each M and m.

Mia met Mary.

Follow the path with M to help Mia meet Mary.

MORE FUN

Wipe the picture clean. Then, follow the path with **m** to show Mia and Mary the way to the park.

© Scholastic Inc.

Circle 8 differences.

Trace each N and n.

Name the newt.

Connect the dots from **A** to **N**. You made a newt!
Give the newt a name that starts with **N**.

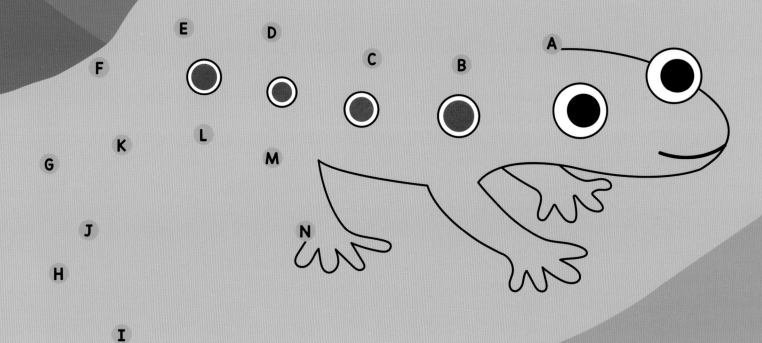

N
_____

Trace each O and o.

Otis is orange.

Draw a line to match each owl with its twin.
Then, find and circle Otis.

Omari

Oliver

Otto

Omri

Orestis

Otis

47

Trace each P and p.

Pedro plays.

Circle the items that begin with the P sound.

Trace each Q and q.

Queenie quilts.

Follow the path with Q and q to help Queenie find her quilt.

DELANEY

Trace each R and r.

Reba races.

Find and circle each R and r in the picture.

How many did you find? R ☐ r ☐

Trace each S and s.

See Sam skate.

Decorate Sam's skateboard with things that start with S. Draw or use stickers.

Trace each T and t.

Tam likes taffy.

Circle the items that begin with the T sound.

Souvenir SHOP

OPEN

TAFFY

© Scholastic Inc.

Draw a line from START to END. What do you see?

START

END

Trace each U and u.

Uma is a unicorn.

Match each unicorn's hair to an umbrella with all the same colors. Then, find and circle Uma.

Ursa

Uri

Uma

Trace each V and v.

Via loves veggies.

Name each item below. Then, write v to finish the word. Circle the vegetables.

___an

___est

___iolin

___egetables

___ase

___ulture

Trace each W and w.

Walrus waddles.

Connect the dots from **A** to **W**. You made a walrus!
Give the walrus a name that starts with **W**.

N WALRUS

W

Trace each X.

X X X X wins.

Play with a friend! Write X in an empty space.
Have a friend write O in a different space. Take turns.
The first player to get 4 Xs or Os in a row →, ↓, or ↘ wins!

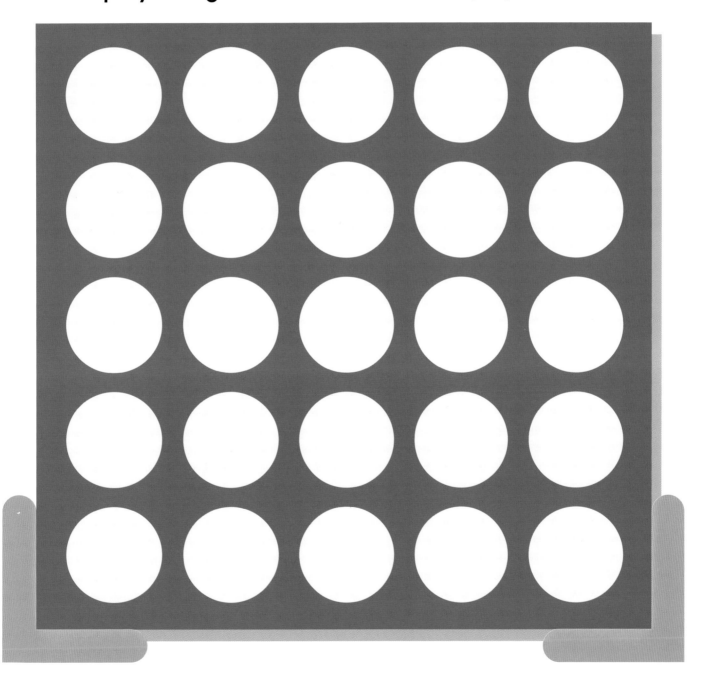

Trace each Y and y.

Yair loves yolks.

Circle the items that begin with the Y sound.

Trace each Z and z.

Zach zigzags.

Circle each Z and z in the picture.

How many did you find?   Z [ ]   z [ ]

© Scholastic Inc.

Draw a monster. Follow the steps in the picture.

1
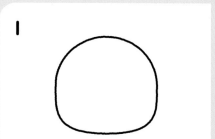

2
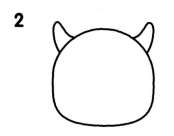

3

4

5

6

Draw more monsters.

Fill in the missing letters on the game board.

START

A B C D E F G

H I J K L M N O P

Q R S T U V W

X Y Z

Circle each consonant in the tree.

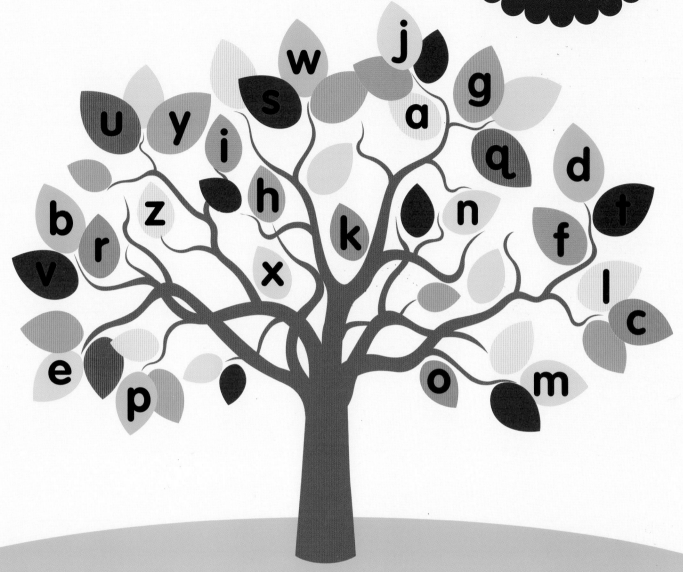

The vowel pictures are missing! Find the stickers. Place them below. Then, trace each vowel.

Trace each short-*a* word.

Vowels have two sounds: short and long. Short a makes the sound you hear in the middle of *tag* and *cap*.

cat   bat

van   can

nap   sat

Read the sentence. Then, write the short-*a* words on the lines below.

The cat sat on the mad bat.

_____   _____

Change bat into cat. Use the clues and letter tiles. Start at the bottom and climb to the top.

t c (m) r n

cat

change the last letter

change the first letter

mat (o l m)

change the first letter

nap (N AP)

change the last letter

rat (Roy)

change the first letter

bat

Circle each picture that makes the short-e sound.

66

Unscramble the short-*e* words on the way to the vet. Use the words in the word bank.

Word Bank

bed   leg   web   red   pen

r d e ___ ___ ___

d b e ___ ___ ___

e l g ___ ___ ___

w b e ___ ___ ___

e n p ___ ___ ___

Make a short-*i* word list! Use the letter tiles and picture clues to build your list.

P I G

G I F T

W I Z G G

F I S H

6   I

f g h k n

p t s w x

Write **b** next to each short-*i* word ending in the tree. If you made a real word, circle it. Then, wipe clean to make new words. Choose letters from the seeds below.

Trace each short-o word.

Read the sentence. Then, write the short-o words on the lines below.

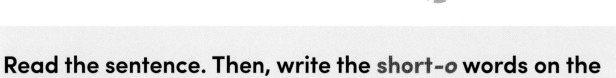

A fox, a hog, and a dog sit on a log.

_____ _____

_____ _____

70

Solve each short-*o* puzzle. Use the pictures and the words in the Word Bank. The first one has been done for you.

Word Bank							
dog	mop	fox	pot	log	box	hot	hog

d o g

© Scholastic Inc.

71

Draw lines to match the duck with the short-*u* words.

skunk

ball

drum

rug

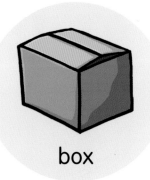
box

wig

mug

nest

bus

hen

72

© Scholastic Inc.

Unscramble each short-_u_ word.

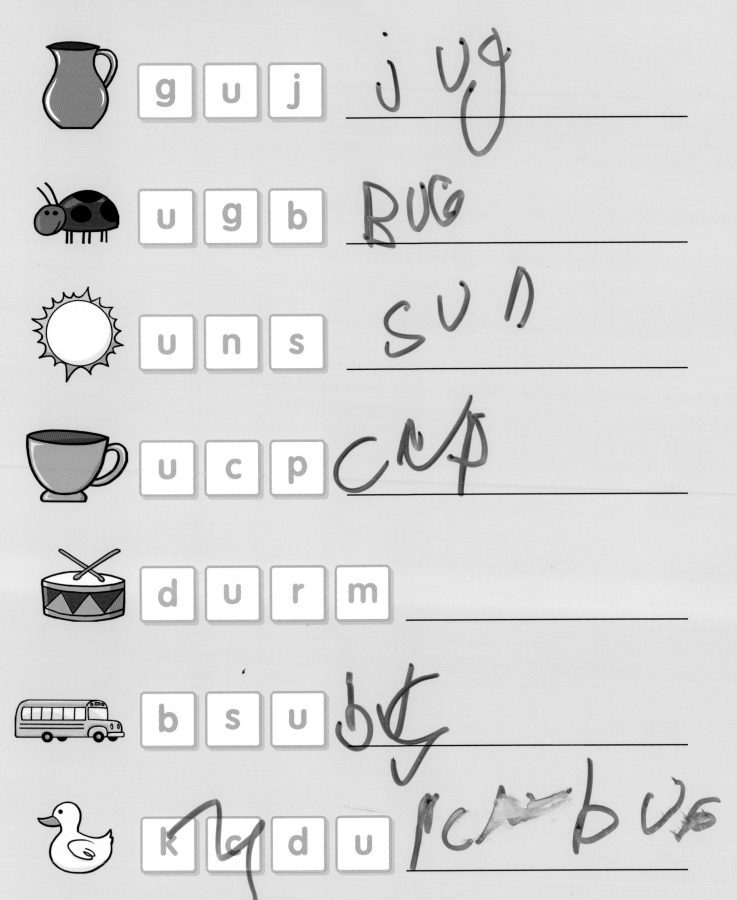

g u j   jug

u g b   BUG

u n s   SUN

u c p   CUP

d u r m

b s u   bus

k c d u

Circle each picture that makes the long-*a* sound.

Make a long-*e* word list! Use the letter tiles and picture clues to build your list.

Key

leaf

seal

tree

Bee

b l s t k f r

Write *e* on the line to change each short-*i* word into a long-*i* word.

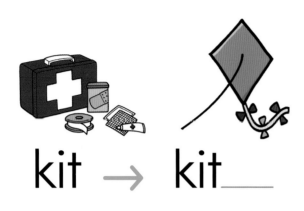

kit → kit___

Tim → tim___

pin → pin___

fin → fin___

Write each long-*i* word from above in the correct boxes.

Solve each long-*o* puzzle.
Use the pictures and the words in the Word Bank.

Help the unicorn find the ukelele.
Circle the words that make the long-u sound.

unicorn

music

boat

bike

cake

unicycle

mule

cube

gate

key

bee

vacuum

ukulele

78

What makes you happy? Draw it.

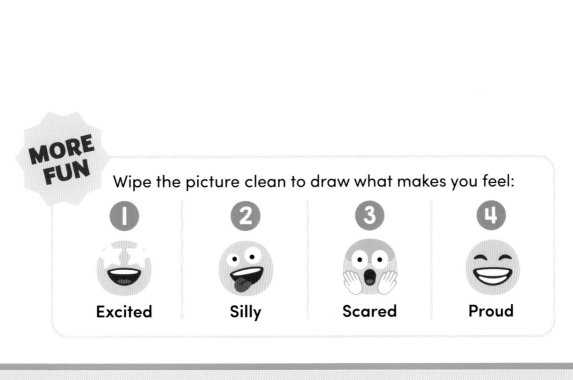

MORE FUN

Wipe the picture clean to draw what makes you feel:

1 Excited
2 Silly
3 Scared
4 Proud

Play long-vowel tic-tac-toe with a friend!
Then, wipe clean and play again.

WORD BANK

boat	tape	five	music
mule	rake	tree	cape
kite	bee	rose	slide
sheep	cube	feet	coat

a e i o u

★ Choose a long-vowel sound: *a, e, i, o,* or *u.*

★ Have your friend choose a different long-vowel sound.

★ Write a word with your vowel-sound in a square.
Use words from the Word Bank or your own.

★ Take turns.

★ The first player to get 3 words in a row →, ↓, or ↘ wins!

Help the children find the path out of the maze.

am

Say it.   **Trace it.**   **Spell it.**

Help the duck get to the nest. Follow the puddles with am.

Complete the sentence about the picture. Write am.

I _____ happy.

 **too**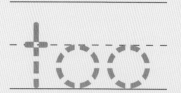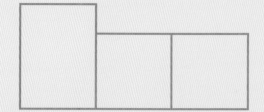

Say it. **Trace it.** **Spell it.**

Trace each raindrop with too.

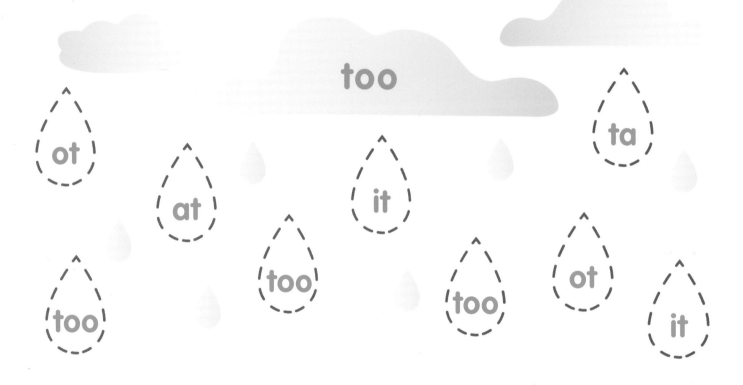

Complete the sentence about the picture. Write too.

We go to school _____.

84

she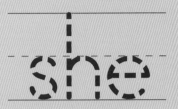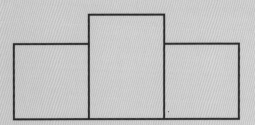

Say it.   **Trace it.**   **Spell it.**

Circle each she.

the   she   we   she

he   are   he

she   tea   are

to   that   she   to

she   she   his   we   she

Complete the sentence about the picture. Write She.

_____ has a dog.

like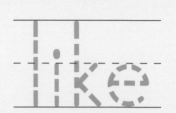

Say it. **Trace it.** **Spell it.**

Find and circle **like** 6 times. Words go → and ↓.

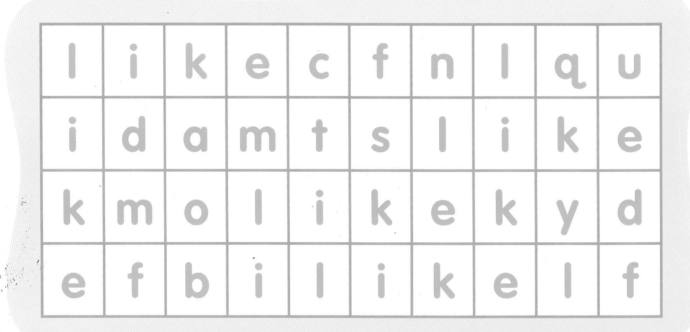

l	i	k	e	c	f	n	l	q	u
i	d	a	m	t	s	l	i	k	e
k	m	o	l	i	k	e	k	y	d
e	f	b	i	l	i	k	e	l	f

Complete the sentence about the picture. Write **like**.

We _____ ice cream.

86

was

was

Say it.   **Trace it.**   **Spell it.**

Help each ball get to its pin. Connect the dots to spell was.

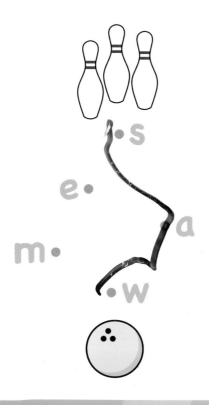
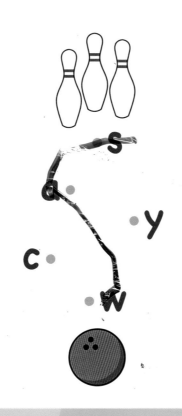
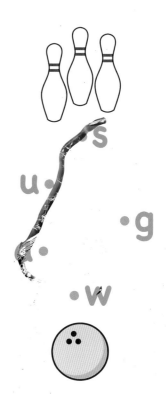

Complete the sentence about the picture. Write was.

Yesterday ____was____ a great day.

that

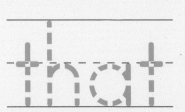

Say it.

Trace it.

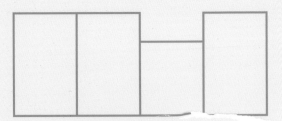

Spell it.

Write the missing letters to spell that.

__h__t

__ __a__

th__ __

t__ __t

Complete the sentence about the picture. Write that.

I think _____ looks fun!

88

© Scholastic Inc.

Circle the object that matches each shape on the left.

Trace each color word. Match each word to the correct color.

red

orange

green

yellow

purple

blue

Read the sentences.
Circle the picture each sentence describes.

That is a red bug.

I see a yellow bus.

Her shirt is blue.

My coat is orange.

What sweater pattern comes next? Draw it.

Make your own pattern. Have a friend draw the last pattern.

Which bead comes next? Draw it.

Make your own bead pattern. Have a friend draw the last bead.

ALL ABOUT

This is me!

My Favorite

Animal: LION

Book: YESno

Color: BLUE

Food: AMERE

I am 5 years old.

I show kindness by

AMNA NANA

I am a star because

I'M 5 YEQRs

Answer Key For pages not shown, please check your child's work.

What goes in Karol's bookbag? Trace each path to find out.

Circle 8 differences.

Count each animal. Write the number.

8 2 1 4 10

Mama Hen has lost her chicks. Find and circle 10 chicks.

Circle the two ice cream cones that are the same.

Trace each B and b.

Ben buys a bike.

Circle the items that begin with the B sound.

Trace each E and e.

Ed exercises.

Find and circle each E and e in the picture.

How many did you find? E 6   e 5

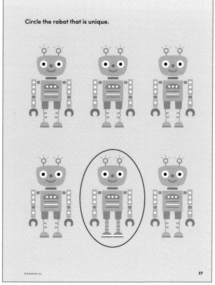

Circle the robot that is unique.

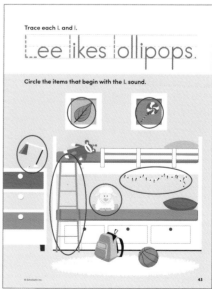

Trace each L and l.

Lee likes lollipops.

Circle the items that begin with the L sound.

Circle 8 differences.

45

Trace each P and p.

Pedro plays.

Circle the items that begin with the P sound.

48

Trace each R and r.

Reba races.

Find and circle each R and r in the picture.

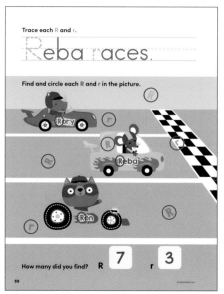

How many did you find? R 7   r 3

50

Trace each T and t.

Tam likes taffy.

Circle the items that begin with the T sound.

52

Draw a line from START to END. What do you see?

53

Trace each Y and y.

Yair loves yolks.

Circle the items that begin with the Y sound.

58

Trace each Z and z.

Zach zigzags.

Circle each Z and z in the picture.

How many did you find? Z 4   z 5

59

Change bat into cat. Use the clues and letter tiles.
Start at the bottom and climb to the top.

t c m r n

cat — change the last letter
can — change the first letter
man — change the first letter
ran — change the last letter
rat — change the first letter
bat

65

Circle each picture that makes the short-e sound.

Short e makes the sound you hear in the middle of pet and yes.

66

Printed in Rawang, Malaysia. PO# 5057717

Illustrations: Doug Jones; Shutterstock Inc. • STK882209